EASY SAUSAGE COOKBOOK

50 DELICIOUS AND EASY SAUSAGE RECIPES

By
Chef Maggie Chow
Copyright © 2015 by Saxonberg Associates

Published by
BookSumo, a division of Saxonberg Associates
http://www.booksumo.com/

INTRODUCTION

Welcome to *The Effortless Chef Series*! Thank you for taking the time to download the *Easy Sausage Cookbook*. Come take a journey with me into the delights of easy cooking. The point of this cookbook and all my cookbooks is to exemplify the effortless nature of cooking simply.

In this book we focus on Sausage. You will find that even though the recipes are simple, the taste of the dishes is quite amazing.

So will you join me in an adventure of simple cooking? If the answer is yes (and I hope it is) please consult the table of contents to find the dishes you are most interested in. Once you are ready jump right in and start cooking.

— Chef Maggie Chow

TABLE OF CONTENTS

Any Issues? Contact Me

If you find that something important to you is missing from this book please contact me at maggie@booksumo.com.

I will try my best to re-publish a revised copy taking your feedback into consideration and let you know when the book has been revised with you in mind.

:)

— Chef Maggie Chow

Legal Notes

COMMON ABBREVIATIONS

cup(s)	C.
tablespoon	tbsp
teaspoon	tsp
ounce	oz.
pound	lb

*All units used are standard American measurements

CHAPTER 1: EASY SAUSAGE RECIPES

GERMAN DUMPLINGS AND SAUSAGE

Ingredients

- 1 1/3 C. all-purpose flour
- 1 tsp salt
- 3 eggs
- 1/3 C. water
- 1 tsp vegetable oil
- 2 slices bacon, diced
- 1/2 large onion, diced
- 2 tbsps butter
- 1 small Gala apple, cored and diced
- 2 tbsps brown sugar
- 1 (16 oz.) package sauerkraut
- 1 (16 oz.) package kielbasa sausage, cut into 2-inch pieces

Directions

- Coat a colander made of metal with oil then set your oven to 350 degrees before doing anything else.
- Get a bowl, combine: salt and flour. Stir the dry mix then combine the water and eggs. Continue mixing everything until you form a dough.
- Get a saucepan of water boiling then put the dough in the colander and place the colander over the pot, once the water is boiling.

- Press the dough out of the colander then let the dough boil.
- Let the dough cook for 6 mins or until you find that the pieces begin to float.
- As the dough floats spoon it out into a casserole dish coated with oil.
- Now begin to fry your bacon when all of the dough has cooked.
- Fry the bacon for 10 mins then place the meat to the side.
- Begin to stir fry your onions in the drippings for 12 mins.
- Get a separate frying pan and melt your butter in it then add in the brown sugar and apple.
- Let the apple cook while stirring it for 7 mins then place the sauerkraut, onions, and bacon in the pan.
- Stir and heat everything for 6 mins then enter everything into the casserole dish over the dough.
- Cook your sausage in the microwave for 4 mins, with the highest heating level, until they are done then place the sausages in the dish as well.
- Cook everything in the oven for 17 mins.
- Enjoy.

Amount per serving (6 total)

Timing Information:

Preparation	25 m
Cooking	55 m
Total Time	1 h 20 m

Nutritional Information:

Calories	496 kcal
Fat	31.7 g
Carbohydrates	34.1g
Protein	17.5 g
Cholesterol	161 mg
Sodium	1644 mg

* Percent Daily Values are based on a 2,000 calorie diet.

LOUISIANA HOMEMADE SAUSAGE

Ingredients

- 1 1/2 yards of large sausage casing, submerged in water for 2 hrs
- 4 lbs lean pork meat, chunked then ground
- 2 lbs pork fat
- 1/4 C. minced garlic
- 2 tbsps salt
- 1 tsp freshly ground black pepper
- 1 tsp cayenne pepper
- 1/4 tsp dried thyme
- 1 tbsp ground paprika
- 1/4 tsp crushed bay leaf
- 1/4 tsp dried sage
- 5 tsps hickory-flavored liquid smoke

Directions

- Get a bowl, combine: hickory smoke, ground meat, sage, salt, bay leaf, pepper, paprika, thyme, and cayenne. Divide your casing into 26 inch pieces then tie a knot on one side. Use a sausage stuffer to fill the sausage with the mix. Leave about 1 inch of space in the sausage and slowly tie another knot into the open end of the casing.
- Dice your sausages into 1/2 inch coins and fry the pieces with no water for 13 mins per side. Enjoy.

Amount per serving (24 total)

Timing Information:

Preparation	20 m
Cooking	15 m
Total Time	1 h 35 m

Nutritional Information:

Calories	482 kcal
Fat	45.8 g
Carbohydrates	0.7g
Protein	< 15.6 g
Cholesterol	72 mg
Sodium	628 mg

* Percent Daily Values are based on a 2,000 calorie diet.

Maggie's Easy Boudin

(Liver Sausage)

Ingredients

- 2 1/2 lbs boneless pork shoulder, cubed
- 1 lb pork liver, cut into pieces
- 4 C. water
- 2 C. uncooked white rice
- 4 C. water
- 1 1/4 C. green onions, diced
- 1 C. diced onion
- 1/2 C. minced celery
- 1 red bell pepper, diced
- 1 C. diced fresh parsley
- 2 tbsps finely diced cilantro
- 1 tsp minced garlic
- 4 tsps salt
- 2 1/2 tsps cayenne pepper
- 1 1/2 tsps ground black pepper
- 1/2 tsp red pepper flakes
- 4 feet 1 1/2 inch diameter hog casings, cleaned thoroughly

Directions

- Get the following boiling in a large pot: 4 C. water, liver, and pork shoulder.
- Once the mix is boiling set the heat to a low / medium level, place a lid on the pot, and cook everything for 90 mins.

- Get your rice boiling in 4 C. of water.
- Once the mix is boiling, set the heat to low, place a lid on the pot, and cook the rice for 22 mins.
- Remove the pork from the pot and place it to the side to lose its heat.
- Add in the following to simmering mix: pepper flakes, green onions, black pepper, diced onions, cayenne, celery, salt, bell pepper, garlic, cilantro, and parsley.
- Let this mix simmer until the onions are soft.
- As the mix is cooking grind your pork then add it to the mix.
- Heat and stir the mix for 12 mins. Then add the cooked rice and shut the heat.
- Stuff the mix into the casing once it is cool enough to handle then perforate each sausage with a needle, a few times, all over.
- Get a saucepan of water and salt boiling then set the heat to a medium level and cook the sausages for 7 mins.
- Enjoy.

Amount per serving (18 total)

Timing Information:

Preparation	30 m
Cooking	2 h
Total Time	3 h 30 m

Nutritional Information:

Calories	188 kcal
Fat	6.6 g
Carbohydrates	20g
Protein	11.2 g
Cholesterol	64 mg
Sodium	551 mg

* Percent Daily Values are based on a 2,000 calorie diet.

THE BEST HOMEMADE HOT DOGS

Ingredients

- 1 1/4 lbs lean ground beef
- 1/4 lb ground pork
- 4 tsps kosher salt
- 1 tbsp paprika
- 2 tsps ground black pepper
- 1 tsp granulated onion powder
- 1 tsp granulated garlic
- 1/2 tsp smoked paprika
- 1/3 C. ice water
- 4 hot dog buns, split and toasted

Directions

- Get a bowl, combine: ice water, beef, smoked paprika, pork, garlic, black pepper, salt, paprika, and onion.
- Work the mix with your hands for 5 mins.
- Cover the bowl with plastic and place everything in the fridge for 3 hrs.
- Lay out a large piece of plastic on a cutting board and keep your hands wet as you complete this step.
- Divide your meat into 4 pieces.
- Lay one piece of the meat on the plastic and shape the meat into a cylinder. Then wrap the plastic around it.

- Now work the meat into a thinner sausage about the length of a hot dog.
- Lay the sausage in a casserole dish covered in plastic.
- Continue forming sausages in this manner and then place everything in the fridge until it is chilled.
- Coat an outdoor grilling grate with oil and get the grill hot.
- Carefully unwrap your sausages and place them on the grill.
- Let them cook for 3 to 4 mins without any turning. Then occasionally turn them.
- Cook the meat for 6 more mins.
- At this point your sausages should be completely done if not continue to cook them.
- Serve your sausages with the buns.
- Enjoy.

Amount per serving (4 total)

Timing Information:

Preparation	15 m
Cooking	10 m
Total Time	2 h 25 m

Nutritional Information:

Calories	461 kcal
Fat	23.5 g
Carbohydrates	24g
Protein	36.6 g
Cholesterol	111 mg
Sodium	2227 mg

* Percent Daily Values are based on a 2,000 calorie diet.

Cajun Stew

Ingredients

- 1/4 C. butter
- 10 oz. andouille sausage, halved lengthwise and cut into 1/4-inch half-moons
- 1 C. diced onion
- 1 C. diced celery
- 1 C. diced green bell pepper
- 1 1/2 tsps minced garlic
- 1 (6 oz.) can tomato paste
- 1 (14.5 oz.) can diced tomatoes
- 2 tsps Worcestershire sauce (such as Lea & Perrins(R))
- 1 1/2 tsps Cajun seasoning, or to taste
- 1/2 tsp ground black pepper
- 4 C. low-sodium chicken broth
- 2 C. medium-grain rice
- 3/4 lb shrimp, peeled and deveined
- 3/4 lb cod fillets, cut into 1 1/2-inch chunks (optional)
- salt to taste
- 1/3 C. diced fresh parsley

Directions

- Fry your sausages for 7 mins in butter then place them to the side.
- Add the bell peppers, celery, and onions to the pan and fry them for 9 mins.

- Add the garlic and cook it for 2 more mins then add the sausage back in with: the black pepper, diced tomatoes, Cajun seasoning, and Worcestershire sauce.
- Combine the mix evenly to distribute the spices and sauce. Then add in the broth and get everything boiling.
- Once the mix is boiling pour in the rice, place a lid on the pot, set the heat to low, and let the contents cook for 27 mins.
- Stir the cod and shrimp into the rice and get everything boiling again. Once the mix is boiling, set the heat to low, and continue cooking the mix for 12 mins.
- Top everything with parsley and salt then stir.
- Enjoy.

Amount per serving (6 total)

Timing Information:

Preparation	30 m
Cooking	1 h 10 m
Total Time	1 h 40 m

Nutritional Information:

Calories	622 kcal
Fat	23 g
Carbohydrates	66.8g
Protein	34.5 g
Cholesterol	157 mg
Sodium	1880 mg

* Percent Daily Values are based on a 2,000 calorie diet.

COUNTRYSIDE SWEET SAUSAGES

Ingredients

- 1/2 C. white sugar
- 1 tsp dried oregano
- 1/4 tsp ground ginger
- 1/2 tsp ground pepper
- 4 1/2 tsps fine salt
- 1/2 tsp curing salt
- 1 tbsp minced garlic
- 2 lbs ground pork
- 1 lb coarse ground pork back fat
- 1/4 C. distilled white vinegar
- Hog casing, cleaned to remove salt

Directions

- Get a bowl, combine: curing salt, sugar, regular salt, oregano, pepper, and ginger.
- Get a 2nd bowl, combine: pork, pork fat, and garlic.
- Combine both bowls then add the vinegar and combine everything again.
- Cut your casing into 3 inch pieces.
- Tie one end of each casing with some kitchen twine then fill the casing.
- Tie the opposite end and place everything into a casserole dish.
- Place a covering of plastic on the dish and put everything in the fridge for 5 days.

- Add about half of an inch of water to a frying pan and cook the sausages with a gentle boil and a medium to high level of heat for 22 mins, with a lid on the pot, then remove the lid and continue to fry the sausages for 9 more mins.
- Enjoy.

Amount per serving (12 total)

Timing Information:

Preparation	45 m
Cooking	28 m
Total Time	4 d 1 h 13 m

Nutritional Information:

Calories	496 kcal
Fat	44.4 g
Carbohydrates	8.7g
Protein	14.6 g
Cholesterol	71 mg
Sodium	1011 mg

* Percent Daily Values are based on a 2,000 calorie diet.

PARMESAN SAUSAGE

Ingredients

- 8 oz. whole wheat rotini pasta
- 3 bunches broccoli rabe, trimmed
- 4 (4 oz.) links hot Italian sausage, cut into 1 inch pieces
- 1 tbsp sausage drippings
- 2 garlic cloves, diced
- 1 (14.5 oz.) can diced tomatoes
- salt and ground black pepper to taste
- 1/2 C. grated Parmesan cheese
- 1/4 tsp crushed red pepper flakes
- 1 tsp olive oil, or to taste

Directions

- Get your pasta boiling in water and salt for 8 mins. Then remove all the liquids.
- Steam your broccoli for 4 mins using a steamer insert. Then begin to fry your sausage for 7 mins until it is fully done.
- Place the sausage to the side and remove some of the oils.
- Add your garlic to the rest of the drippings and fry everything for 2 mins then add 1/2 of the broccoli rabe.

- Fry the rabe until it is soft then stir in the diced tomatoes.
- Let everything cook for 7 mins then top the mix with black pepper and salt.
- Add the sausage back in and heat it up.
- Now top everything with olive oil, parmesan, and red pepper flakes.
- Liberally top your pasta with the sauce.
- Enjoy.

Amount per serving (4 total)

Timing Information:

Preparation	15 m
Cooking	15 m
Total Time	30 m

Nutritional Information:

Calories	605 kcal
Fat	28.3 g
Carbohydrates	55.5g
Protein	34.6 g
Cholesterol	73 mg
Sodium	1089 mg

* Percent Daily Values are based on a 2,000 calorie diet.

ITALIAN PASTA

Ingredients

- 1 (16 oz.) package dry ziti pasta
- 1 lb mild Italian sausage
- 1 (15 oz.) container ricotta cheese
- 1 egg
- 1 large yellow onion, minced
- 2 tsps minced garlic
- 1 tsp dried oregano
- 1/2 tsp salt
- 1/2 tsp ground black pepper
- 1 1/2 (26 oz.) jars spaghetti sauce, divided
- 1 (8 oz.) package shredded Italian cheese blend
- 1 tsp dried basil (optional)

Directions

- Coat a casserole dish with oil then set your oven to 350 degrees before doing anything else.
- Get your ziti boiling in water for 9 mins then remove the liquids.
- At the same time fry your sausage for 12 mins until it is fully done.
- Get a bowl, combine: oregano, ricotta, garlic, onion, and eggs.
- Combine the mix until it is smooth then add the pasta, half of the pasta sauce, sausage, pepper, and salt.

- Pour one third of the pasta sauce into the casserole dish then add half of the ziti mix, one third of the pasta sauce, half of the cheese, the rest of the pasta, one third of the sauce, and half of the cheese.
- Top everything with basil and add any remaining ingredients.
- Place a covering of foil on the dish and cook everything in oven for 22 mins.
- Now remove the foil and continue cooking the dish for 7 more mins.
- Enjoy.

Amount per serving (8 total)

Timing Information:

Preparation	30 m
Cooking	30 m
Total Time	1 h

Nutritional Information:

Calories	649 kcal
Fat	27.4 g
Carbohydrates	68.9g
Protein	30.7 g
Cholesterol	86 mg
Sodium	1485 mg

* Percent Daily Values are based on a 2,000 calorie diet.

TUSCAN SOUP

Ingredients

- 1 lb bulk mild Italian sausage
- 1 1/4 tsps crushed red pepper flakes
- 4 slices bacon, cut into 1/2 inch pieces
- 1 large onion, diced
- 1 tbsp minced garlic
- 5 (13.75 oz.) cans chicken broth
- 6 potatoes, thinly sliced
- 1 C. heavy cream
- 1/4 bunch fresh spinach, tough stems removed

Directions

- Fry your sausages for 13 mins then remove a majority of the excess oils.
- Begin to fry your bacon for 12 mins. Then add in the onions and stir fry them for 4 mins.
- Now add in the broth and get everything boiling.
- Once the mix is boiling stir in the potatoes and cook everything for 22 mins.
- Turn the heat down a bit then combine in the cream.
- Get the cream completely mixed in then add the spinach and let the leaves cook for 3 more mins. Enjoy.

Amount per serving (6 total)

Timing Information:

Preparation	25 m
Cooking	1 h
Total Time	1 h 25 m

Nutritional Information:

Calories	554 kcal
Fat	32.6 g
Carbohydrates	45.8g
Protein	19.8 g
Cholesterol	99 mg
Sodium	2386 mg

* Percent Daily Values are based on a 2,000 calorie diet.

KALE STEW

Ingredients

- 1 C. dry navy beans, soak in water for 8 hours
- 1 large bunch kale, rinsed, stemmed and diced
- 1 tbsp olive oil
- 1 lb spicy linguica sausage, sliced
- 1 C. diced shallots
- 4 C. chicken broth
- salt and pepper to taste
- 1/2 tsp hot sauce, or to taste

Directions

- Remove your beans from the liquid and place them in a pressure cooker with 4 C. of fresh water for 30 mins, then release the pressure of the cooker.
- At the same time begin to boil your kale in water and salt for 4 mins then remove all the liquids.
- For 6 mins brown your sausage, place them to side, and fry your shallots for 4 mins.
- Add in some broth and scrape the bottom of the pan, then add the sausages and beans into the mix.

- Add the rest of the broth as well, the hot sauce, some pepper, and some salt.
- Stir the mix and get everything boiling.
- Once the mix is boiling set the heat to low and gently cook everything for 17 mins.
- Now add in the kale and get it hot.
- Enjoy.

Amount per serving (8 total)

Timing Information:

Preparation	15 m
Cooking	1 h
Total Time	9 h 15 m

Nutritional Information:

Calories	373 kcal
Fat	23.8 g
Carbohydrates	20.3g
Protein	19.2 g
Cholesterol	50 mg
Sodium	775 mg

* Percent Daily Values are based on a 2,000 calorie diet.

ADVANCED LASAGNA

Ingredients

- 1 lb sweet Italian sausage
- 3/4 lb lean ground beef
- 1/2 C. minced onion
- 2 cloves garlic, crushed
- 1 (28 oz.) can crushed tomatoes
- 2 (6 oz.) cans tomato paste
- 2 (6.5 oz.) cans canned tomato sauce
- 1/2 C. water
- 2 tbsps white sugar
- 1 1/2 tsps dried basil leaves
- 1/2 tsp fennel seeds
-

- 1 tsp Italian seasoning
- 1 tbsp salt
- 1/4 tsp ground black pepper
- 4 tbsps diced fresh parsley
- 12 lasagna noodles
- 16 oz. ricotta cheese
- 1 egg
- 1/2 tsp salt
- 3/4 lb mozzarella cheese, sliced
- 3/4 C. grated Parmesan cheese

Directions

- Get a large pot and begin to fry your garlic, onions, beef, and sausage until everything is browned nicely then add in the water, crushed tomatoes, tomato sauce, and tomato paste.
- Stir the mix evenly then add half of the parsley, pepper, and 1 tbsp of salt.
- Stir the mix again and let the contents gently boil for 90 mins.
- Continue to stir every 15 mins.
- Get your pasta boiling in water and salt for 9 mins then remove all the liquids.
- Get a bowl, combine: 1/2 tsp salt, ricotta, the rest of the parsley, and the eggs.
- Stir the mix until it is smooth then set your oven to 375 degrees before doing anything else.
- Layer 1.5 C. of sauce on the bottom of a casserole dish then layer six pieces of lasagna.
- Add half of the ricotta mix, 1/3 of mozzarella, 1.5 C. of sauce, and 1/4 C. of parmesan.
- Continue layering in this manner until all the ingredients have been used up.
- Place a covering of foil on the dish that has been coated with nonstick spray and cook everything for 30 mins in the oven.
- Take off the foil and continue cooking everything for 17 more mins.
- Enjoy.

Amount per serving (12 total)

Timing Information:

Preparation	30 m
Cooking	2 h 30 m
Total Time	3 h 15 m

Nutritional Information:

Calories	448 kcal
Fat	21.3 g
Carbohydrates	36.5g
Protein	29.7 g
Cholesterol	82 mg
Sodium	1788 mg

* Percent Daily Values are based on a 2,000 calorie diet.

SEATTLE ARTISANAL ZUCCHINI

Ingredients

- 2 zucchini, ends trimmed
- 3 tbsps olive oil
- 2 links Italian-style chicken sausage, casings removed
- 2 tsps crushed red pepper flakes (optional)
- salt and ground black pepper to taste
- 1/2 sweet onion (such as Vidalia(R)), diced
- 3 cloves garlic, diced
- 1 (14.5 oz.) can whole peeled tomatoes, drained and diced
- 1/2 C. dry bread crumbs
- 1/4 C. grated Parmesan cheese
- 1 tbsp diced fresh basil

Directions

- Set your oven to 375 degrees before doing anything else.
- Cut an inch long slice from each zucchini to remove the insides. Save the insides of the veggie for another recipe. Your zucchini should be in the shape of a boat.
- Now dice the portions of the zucchini that you sliced and place them to the side.

- Begin to fry your sausage in olive oil for 10 mins then add in some pepper, salt and the pepper flakes. Stir the mix then add the garlic, onions, and diced zucchini. Let the veggies cook for 7 mins then put everything in bowl. Combine with the mix: basil, tomatoes, parmesan, and bread crumbs.
- Work the mix until everything is completely mixed then gently fill your zucchini with it. Layer everything into a casserole dish. For 35 mins cook the zucchinis in the oven.
- Enjoy.

Amount per serving (4 total)

Timing Information:

Preparation	20 m
Cooking	45 m
Total Time	1 h 5 m

Nutritional Information:

Calories	260 kcal
Fat	15.7 g
Carbohydrates	20g
Protein	11.7 g
Cholesterol	37 mg
Sodium	548 mg

* Percent Daily Values are based on a 2,000 calorie diet.

Italian Pasta II

Ingredients

- 1 (12 oz.) package bow tie pasta
- 2 tbsps olive oil
- 1 lb sweet Italian sausage, casings removed and crumbled
- 1/2 tsp red pepper flakes
- 1/2 C. diced onion
- 3 cloves garlic, minced
- 1 (28 oz.) can Italian-style plum tomatoes, drained and coarsely diced
- 1 1/2 C. heavy cream
- 1/2 tsp salt
- 3 tbsps minced fresh parsley

Directions

- Get your pasta boiling in water and salt for 9 mins then remove all the liquids. Begin to fry your sausage in oil then add in the pepper flakes as well as the sausage.
- Fry the meat until it is browned all over. Then add in your garlic and onions. Fry them until the onions are soft.
- Now add in the salt, cream, and tomatoes.
- Get the mix gently boiling and cook everything for 12 mins.
- Now add some parsley, stir the mix, then add the pasta and stir everything again. Enjoy.

Amount per serving (6 total)

Timing Information:

Preparation	15 m
Cooking	30 m
Total Time	45 m

Nutritional Information:

Calories	656 kcal
Fat	42.1 g
Carbohydrates	50.9g
Protein	20.1 g
Cholesterol	111 mg
Sodium	1088 mg

* Percent Daily Values are based on a 2,000 calorie diet.

COATED PORK SAUSAGES

Ingredients

- 1 lb pork sausage
- 1 onion, finely diced
- 1 green bell pepper, finely diced
- 1 tsp crushed red pepper flakes
- 2 tbsps garlic, minced
- 4 tbsps unsalted butter
- salt and pepper to taste
- 4 tbsps all-purpose flour
- 1 tsp minced fresh sage
- 1 tsp minced fresh thyme
- 2 C. milk, divided
- 2 cubes chicken bouillon
- 1/4 C. minced fresh parsley

Directions

- Begin to stir fry the following: garlic, pork, pepper flakes, green pepper, and onions.
- Once the pork is fully done remove a majority the excess oil.
- Add in the pepper, salt, and butter to the mix and once the butter has melted add in your flour.
- Combine everything and let the mix cook for 7 mins.
- Make sure to continually stir the mix for these 7 mins.
- Now add the thyme and sage and then add the milk slowly.

- Add your milk half a C. at a time and let it thicken for a few secs then add in more milk.
- Add some more pepper and salt then add another 1/4 C. of milk and the parsley.
- Enjoy.

Amount per serving (4 total)

Timing Information:

Preparation	15 m
Cooking	20 m
Total Time	35 m

Nutritional Information:

Calories	700 kcal
Fat	60.1 g
Carbohydrates	20.3g
Protein	19.7 g
Cholesterol	118 mg
Sodium	1389 mg

* Percent Daily Values are based on a 2,000 calorie diet.

Sausage Dump Dinner

Ingredients

- 8 (4 oz.) links fresh Italian sausage
- 1 (26 oz.) jar spaghetti sauce
- 1 green bell pepper, seeded and sliced into strips
- 1 onion, sliced
- 6 hoagie rolls, split lengthwise (optional)

Directions

- Add the following to the crock of a slow cooker: onion, sausage, green pepper, and sauce.
- Combine the mix evenly then place the lid on the slow cooker.
- Let everything cook for 6 hrs with a low level of heat.
- Evenly divide the mix between your rolls.
- Enjoy.

Amount per serving (6 total)

Timing Information:

Preparation	5 m
Cooking	6 h
Total Time	6 h 5 m

Nutritional Information:

Calories	1024 kcal
Fat	57.4 g
Carbohydrates	88.2g
Protein	35.5 g
Cholesterol	117 mg
Sodium	2356 mg

* Percent Daily Values are based on a 2,000 calorie diet.

New York Style Penne

Ingredients

- 1 (12 oz.) package dry penne pasta
- 2 tsps olive oil
- 1 lb mild Italian sausage
- 1 C. diced onion
- 1/2 C. white wine
- 1 (15 oz.) can tomato sauce
- 1 (14.5 oz.) can diced tomatoes with garlic
- 1 (6 oz.) can tomato paste
- 2 C. shredded mozzarella cheese

Directions

- Set your oven to 350 degrees before doing anything else.
- Get your pasta boiling in water and salt for 9 mins then remove all the liquids.
- Begin to fry your onion and sausage, in oil, until the sausage is browned, then remove the liquids.
- Add the wine and let the mix heat for 2 mins while scraping the pan then add in the tomato paste, diced tomatoes, and tomato sauce.
- Stir the mix again evenly then get everything boiling.
- Once the mix is boiling, set the heat to low, and let the contents gently simmer for 12 mins.

- Pour in the pasta to the mix and stir everything, then place the mix in a casserole dish.
- Top the pasta with the mozzarella and cook the penne in the oven for 25 mins.
- Enjoy.

Amount per serving (6 total)

Timing Information:

Preparation	15 m
Cooking	35 m
Total Time	50 m

Nutritional Information:

Calories	664 kcal
Fat	33.5 g
Carbohydrates	59.2g
Protein	31 g
Cholesterol	82 mg
Sodium	1714 mg

* Percent Daily Values are based on a 2,000 calorie diet.

RUSTIC SPINACH PASTA

Ingredients

- 3/4 lb pasta
- 1 tbsp olive oil
- 1 lb spicy Italian sausage
- 1 onion, diced
- 4 cloves garlic, minced
- 1 (14.5 oz.) can chicken broth
- 1 tsp dried basil
- 1 (14.5 oz.) can diced tomatoes
- 1 (10 oz.) package frozen diced spinach
- 1/2 C. grated Parmesan cheese

Directions

- Get your pasta boiling in water and salt for 9 mins then remove all the liquids.
- Being to fry your sausages in oil until they are fully done.
- Add in your onions when a bit of frying time is left before the sausage is completely cooked to fry the garlic and onions alongside the sausage. '
- Let the onions cook for about 6 mins.
- Add the tomatoes, basil, and broth and let the mix cook for 7 mins.
- Combine in the spinach and place a lid on the pot.
- Set the heat to low and let the mix cook.

- Once the spinach is soft stir the pasta into the broth and top everything with cheese.
- Enjoy.

Amount per serving (6 total)

Timing Information:

Preparation	15 m
Cooking	30 m
Total Time	45 m

Nutritional Information:

Calories	423 kcal
Fat	19.3 g
Carbohydrates	39g
Protein	22.3 g
Cholesterol	89 mg
Sodium	1077 mg

* Percent Daily Values are based on a 2,000 calorie diet.

POLISH SAUSAGE AND CABBAGE

Ingredients

- 6 slices bacon
- 1/4 C. water
- 2 tbsps white sugar
- 1 onion, diced
- 2 tsps minced garlic
- 1/4 tsp crushed red pepper flakes
- 1/4 tsp seasoning salt
- 3 tsps caraway seed
- 1 large head cabbage, cut into small wedges
- 1 lb Polish kielbasa

Directions

- Fry your bacon until fully done then remove them from the pan.
- Add the following to the bacon: caraway, water, seasoned salt, onions, pepper flakes, sugar and garlic.
- Stir the mix to evenly distribute the spices then add in the cabbage and stir everything again.
- Place a lid on the pan and let the mix cook for 13 mins with a low to medium level of heating.
- Now combine in the sausage and place the lid back on the pan again.

- Let the mix continue to cook for 12 more mins then break your bacon into pieces and evenly combine in the pieces.
- Enjoy.

Amount per serving (6 total)

Timing Information:

Preparation	10 m
Cooking	30 m
Total Time	40 m

Nutritional Information:

Calories	377 kcal
Fat	26 g
Carbohydrates	20.2g
Protein	17.2 g
Cholesterol	63 mg
Sodium	952 mg

* Percent Daily Values are based on a 2,000 calorie diet.

Maggie's Favorite Jambalaya

Ingredients

- 2 tsps olive oil
- 2 boneless skinless chicken breasts, cut into bite-size pieces
- 8 oz. kielbasa, diced
- 1 onion, diced
- 1 green bell pepper, diced
- 1/2 C. diced celery
- 2 tbsps diced garlic
- 1/4 tsp cayenne pepper
- 1/2 tsp onion powder
- salt and ground black pepper to taste
- 2 C. uncooked white rice
- 4 C. chicken stock
- 3 bay leaves
- 2 tsps Worcestershire sauce
- 1 tsp hot pepper sauce

Directions

- Stir fry your sausage and chicken for 7 mins then add in the garlic, onions, celery, and bell peppers.
- Top the veggies with some pepper, salt, onion powder, and cayenne.
- Stir the mix and continue frying everything for 7 more mins.
- Add in your rice and toast the kernels for a min then add the bay leaves and chicken stock.

- Get everything boiling, place a lid on the pan, set the heat to low, and let the rice gently cook for 22 mins.
- Now add in the hot sauce, and Worcestershire.
- Enjoy.

Amount per serving (6 total)

Timing Information:

Preparation	15 m
Cooking	30 m
Total Time	45 m

Nutritional Information:

Calories	488 kcal
Fat	13.8 g
Carbohydrates	58.5g
Protein	29.1 g
Cholesterol	74 mg
Sodium	1082 mg

* Percent Daily Values are based on a 2,000 calorie diet.

SAUSAGE IN THE MORNING

Ingredients

- 2 tsps dried sage
- 2 tsps salt
- 1 tsp ground black pepper
- 1/4 tsp dried marjoram
- 1 tbsp brown sugar
- 1/8 tsp crushed red pepper flakes
- 1 pinch ground cloves
- 2 lbs ground pork

Directions

- Get a bowl, combine: cloves, sage, red pepper, salt, brown sugar, black pepper, and marjoram.
- Stir the spices evenly then add in the pork.
- Work the contents by hand then shape everything into burgers.
- Fry each burger for 7 mins each side.
- Enjoy.

Amount per serving (6 total)

Timing Information:

Preparation	10 m
Cooking	15 m
Total Time	25 m

Nutritional Information:

Calories	409 kcal
Fat	32.2 g
Carbohydrates	2.7g
Protein	< 25.6 g
Cholesterol	109 mg
Sodium	861 mg

* Percent Daily Values are based on a 2,000 calorie diet.

BAKED VEGGIES AND SAUSAGE

Ingredients

- 2 tsps olive oil
- 2 lbs Italian sausage links, cut into 2-inch pieces
- 1/4 C. olive oil
- 4 large potatoes, peeled and thickly sliced
- 2 large green bell peppers, seeded and cut into wedges
- 2 large red bell peppers, seeded and cut into wedges
- 3 large onions, cut into wedges
- 1/2 C. white wine
- 1/2 C. chicken stock
- 1 tsp Italian seasoning
- salt and pepper to taste

Directions

- Set your oven to 400 degrees before doing anything else.
- Now begin to fry your sausages in olive oil (2 tsps). Once they are done place them in a casserole dish.
- Add 1/4 C. of additional oil to the pan and fry your potatoes for 12 mins.
- Stir the potatoes every 2 to 4 mins. Then layer them in the dish as well.
- Add in the onions and bell peppers to the oil and fry them for 7 mins then place them in the casserole dish too.
- Top the contents of the dish with pepper, salt, and the Italian seasoning.

- Then add in your chicken stock and wine.
- Stir the mix slowly then cook everything in the oven for 22 mins.
- Enjoy.

Amount per serving (8 total)

Timing Information:

Preparation	20 m
Cooking	45 m
Total Time	1 h 5 m

Nutritional Information:

Calories	539 kcal
Fat	29.8 g
Carbohydrates	45.8g
Protein	20.2 g
Cholesterol	45 mg
Sodium	1041 mg

* Percent Daily Values are based on a 2,000 calorie diet.

Portuguese Black Beans

Ingredients

- 1 large squash, halved and seeded
- 1 C. water
- 1/2 (1 lb) chorizo sausage
- 1 tbsp olive oil
- 1 C. diced onion
- 1 clove garlic, minced
- 1/2 green bell pepper, diced
- 1 large tomato, diced
- 1 C. chicken stock
- 1 C. black beans
- 1/2 C. corn
- 1 oz. shredded Cheddar cheese

Directions

- Set your oven to 350 degrees before doing anything else.
- Lay your pieces of squash into a casserole dish and add in some water. For 35 mins cook the veggies in the oven.
- At the same time begin to fry your sausage for 8 mins them remove the excess oils.
- Get another pan and begin to stir fry your garlic and onions for 12 mins then add in the bell pepper and cook them for 5 mins.
- Stir the mix then add in the corn, tomatoes, black beans, and chicken stock.

- Let everything cook for 12 mins while occasionally stirring until all the liquid has cooked out mostly.
- Stuff your squashes with the tomato mix evenly then divide the cheese between each.
- Heat the squash in the oven for 7 mins until the cheese is bubbly.
- Enjoy.

Amount per serving (4 total)

Timing Information:

Preparation	15 m
Cooking	45 m
Total Time	1 h

Nutritional Information:

Calories	532 kcal
Fat	28.7 g
Carbohydrates	42g
Protein	27.9 g
Cholesterol	59 mg
Sodium	997 mg

* Percent Daily Values are based on a 2,000 calorie diet.

GERMAN STYLE APPLES AND SAUSAGE

Ingredients

- 2 lbs sauerkraut, rinsed and drained
- 1 tbsp caraway seeds (optional)
- 1/4 C. brown sugar
- 1 apple, diced
- 1/2 lb bacon, cut into 1-inch pieces
- 1 large onion, diced
- 1 1/2 lbs kielbasa sausage, cut into 1-inch thick slices

Directions

- Get the following boiling: apples, sauerkraut, sugar, and caraway.
- Once it is boiling set the heat to low and let the contents cook for 120 mins.
- Stir the mix at least 3 or 4 times.
- Coat a casserole dish with oil and then set your oven to 350 degrees before doing anything else.
- Stir fry your onions and bacon for 12 mins then pour it into the sauerkraut mix.
- Now stir fry your sausage in the drippings for 13 mins then add it in with the rest of the ingredients.

- Now add everything into a baking dish and cook the mix in the oven for 65 mins.
- Enjoy.

Amount per serving (5 total)

Timing Information:

Preparation	15 m
Cooking	3 h 20 m
Total Time	3 h 35 m

Nutritional Information:

Calories	777 kcal
Fat	62.3 g
Carbohydrates	28.6g
Protein	24.6 g
Cholesterol	128 mg
Sodium	2702 mg

* Percent Daily Values are based on a 2,000 calorie diet.

STIR FRIED SAUERKRAUT

Ingredients

- 2 tbsps butter
- 1 onion, sliced
- 2 cloves garlic, minced
- 1 C. water
- 2 potatoes, sliced
- 1 C. sliced carrots
- 2 tbsps beef bouillon granules
- 1 tsp white sugar
- 1/2 tsp caraway seeds
- 1 (14.5 oz.) can sauerkraut, drained
- 1 lb kielbasa sausage
- 2 tsps all-purpose flour
- 1 C. sour cream
- salt and black pepper to taste

Directions

- Stir fry your garlic and onions in butter for 7 mins then add the following to the mix: caraway, water, sugar, potatoes, bouillon, carrots.
- Get the mix boiling, set the heat to low, and gently cook everything for 17 mins. Add the sauerkraut over the contents in the pot and lay the sausage over everything. Place a lid on the pot and continue cooking the mix for 17 mins. Get a bowl, combine: sour cream and flour.

- Once the mix is smooth combine it with the mix in the pot. Get everything boiling again for a few mins then add some pepper and salt to taste.
- Enjoy.

Amount per serving (6 total)

Timing Information:

Preparation	15 m
Cooking	45 m
Total Time	1 h

Nutritional Information:

Calories	447 kcal
Fat	33 g
Carbohydrates	25.1g
Protein	13.5 g
Cholesterol	77 mg
Sodium	1640 mg

* Percent Daily Values are based on a 2,000 calorie diet.

TOMATO AND BROTH ZUPPA

Ingredients

- 1 lb kielbasa sausage, cut into 1 inch pieces
- 1 tbsp butter
- 1 (14 oz.) can beef broth
- 1 (10.75 oz.) can tomato soup
- 1 1/2 C. water
- 3 C. shredded cabbage
- 1 onion, diced
- 1/2 C. diced green bell pepper
- 1 1/2 tsps salt
- 1/2 tsp ground black pepper
- 1/4 C. sour cream

Directions

- Fry your sausages, in butter, in a big pot, until fully done then add them to the water, pepper, tomato soup, salt, onions, bell pepper, cabbage, and broth.
- Get everything boiling, set the heat to low, and let the contents cook for 50 mins.
- Now add the sour cream and stir the mix.
- Enjoy.

Amount per serving (6 total)

Timing Information:

Preparation	10 m
Cooking	50 m
Total Time	1 h

Nutritional Information:

Calories	297 kcal
Fat	24.8 g
Carbohydrates	7.5g
Protein	11.1 g
Cholesterol	59 mg
Sodium	1517 mg

* Percent Daily Values are based on a 2,000 calorie diet.

Cajun Kielbasa and Rice

Ingredients

- 2 C. water
- 1 C. uncooked rice
- 1 (16 oz.) package turkey kielbasa, cut diagonally into 1/4 inch slices
- 1 onion, diced
- 1 green bell pepper, diced
- 1 clove diced garlic
- 2 (15 oz.) cans canned kidney beans, drained
- 1 (16 oz.) can whole peeled tomatoes, diced
- 1/2 tsp dried oregano
- salt to taste
- 1/2 tsp pepper

Directions

- Get your rice boiling in water.
- Once the mix is boiling, place a lid on the pot, set the heat to low, and let the rice cook for 22 mins.
- At the same time begin to fry your sausage for 7 mins, then add in the garlic, green pepper, and onions.
- Once the onions are soft add in the tomatoes with liquid and the beans.
- Stir the mix evenly then add in some pepper, salt, and the oregano.
- Stir the mix again and let everything cook for 22 mins.

- Lay your rice on a serving plate then liberally top the rice with your bean mix.
- Enjoy.

Amount per serving (8 total)

Timing Information:

Preparation	10 m
Cooking	30 m
Total Time	40 m

Nutritional Information:

Calories	289 kcal
Fat	5.7 g
Carbohydrates	42.4g
Protein	16.3 g
Cholesterol	35 mg
Sodium	808 mg

* Percent Daily Values are based on a 2,000 calorie diet.

Artisan Lentil Dump Dinner

Ingredients

- 1 (16 oz.) package dry lentils
- 1 (16 oz.) can diced tomatoes, drained
- 2 (14 oz.) cans beef broth
- 3 C. water
- 1 carrot, diced
- 2 lbs kielbasa (Polish) sausage, cut into 1/2 inch pieces
- 1 stalk celery, diced

Directions

- Run some fresh water over your lentils then place them in a crock pot with: the celery, tomatoes, sausage, broth, carrots, and water.
- Place a lid on the slow cooker and let the contents cook for 3 hours on high or 8 hours on low.
- Stir the dish then serve it.
- Enjoy.

Amount per serving (12 total)

Timing Information:

Preparation	15 m
Cooking	3 h
Total Time	3 h 15 m

Nutritional Information:

Calories	357 kcal
Fat	21.2 g
Carbohydrates	22.8g
Protein	18.8 g
Cholesterol	50 mg
Sodium	966 mg

* Percent Daily Values are based on a 2,000 calorie diet.

Eastern European Kielbasa

Ingredients

- 4 potatoes, peeled and cut into 1 inch cubes
- 1 onion, diced
- 2 green bell peppers, cut into 1 inch pieces
- 1/2 tsp onion powder
- 1/2 tsp garlic powder
- 1/2 tsp salt
- 1/4 tsp black pepper
- 1/4 C. vegetable oil
- 1 (16 oz.) package kielbasa sausage, cut into 1 inch pieces

Directions

- Let your potatoes and onions gently fry in oil for 17 mins.
- Stir the mix every 3 to 4 mins to avoid any burning then set the heat to low and add your black pepper, bell pepper, salt, garlic powder, and onion powder.
- Place a lid on the pan and let the contents cook for 7 mins.
- Now add in the sausage and place the lid back on the pan.
- Let the sausage cook with a low heat for 17 more mins.
- Enjoy.

Amount per serving (4 total)

Timing Information:

Preparation	15 m
Cooking	35 m
Total Time	50 m

Nutritional Information:

Calories	660 kcal
Fat	44.9 g
Carbohydrates	46.3g
Protein	19.1 g
Cholesterol	75 mg
Sodium	1333 mg

* Percent Daily Values are based on a 2,000 calorie diet.

Mexican Chorizo

Ingredients

- 4 eggs, whisked with 3 tbsps of milk
- 2 high fiber, whole wheat tortillas, sliced into 1/2-inch strips
- 2 oz. dry chorizo sausage, diced
- 2 slices pepper jack cheese
- salt and ground black pepper to taste
- 1 tbsp diced fresh chives

Directions

- Begin to fry your sausage and tortillas for 7 mins then layer your pieces of cheese over the mix then add in the eggs.
- Set the heat to low and begin to gently swirl the mix as it cooks for 6 mins.
- Add some pepper and salt then top the entire dish with some chives when serving it.
- Enjoy.

Amount per serving (2 total)

Timing Information:

Preparation	5 m
Cooking	10 m
Total Time	15 m

Nutritional Information:

Calories	424 kcal
Fat	26 g
Carbohydrates	28.1g
Protein	26.4 g
Cholesterol	412 mg
Sodium	1801 mg

* Percent Daily Values are based on a 2,000 calorie diet.

Soup from San Paolo

Ingredients

- 1 tbsp canola oil
- 1/4 lb chorizo sausage, diced
- 1/3 lb cooked ham, diced
- 1 medium onion, diced
- 2 cloves garlic, minced
- 2 (1 lb) sweet potatoes, peeled and diced
- 1 large red bell pepper, diced
- 2 (14.5 oz.) cans diced tomatoes with juice
- 1 small hot green chile pepper, diced
- 1 1/2 C. water
- 2 (16 oz.) cans black beans, rinsed and drained
- 1 mango - peeled, seeded and diced
- 1/4 C. diced fresh cilantro
- 1/4 tsp salt

Directions

- Stir fry your ham and chorizo for 5 mins then add the garlic and onions and fry them until they are soft.
- Add in: water, sweet potatoes, chili pepper, bell peppers, and tomatoes and liquid.
- Get everything boiling and then place a lid on the pot.
- Set the heat to low and let the contents cook for 17 mins.

- Now add the beans and heat them with no cover on the pot.
- Then add the cilantro and mango.
- Enjoy.

Amount per serving (6 total)

Timing Information:

Preparation	15 m
Cooking	30 m
Total Time	45 m

Nutritional Information:

Calories	508 kcal
Fat	15 g
Carbohydrates	70.7g
Protein	22.8 g
Cholesterol	31 mg
Sodium	1538 mg

* Percent Daily Values are based on a 2,000 calorie diet.

Easy Paella

Ingredients

- 2 tbsps olive oil
- 1 tbsp paprika
- 2 tsps dried oregano
- salt and black pepper to taste
- 2 lbs skinless, boneless chicken breasts, cut into 2 inch pieces
- 2 tbsps olive oil, divided
- 3 cloves garlic, crushed
- 1 tsp crushed red pepper flakes
- 2 C. uncooked short-grain white rice
- 1 pinch saffron threads
- 1 bay leaf
- 1/2 bunch Italian flat leaf parsley, diced
- 1 quart chicken stock
- 2 lemons, zested
- 2 tbsps olive oil
- 1 Spanish onion, diced
- 1 red bell pepper, coarsely diced
- 1 lb chorizo sausage, casings removed and crumbled
- 1 lb shrimp, peeled and deveined

Directions

- Get bowl, combine: pepper, 2 tbsps of olive oil, salt, oregano, and paprika.

- Add the chicken and stir the contents.
- Place a covering of plastic around the bowl and place everything in the fridge.
- Now begin to stir fry your rice, pepper flakes, and garlic in 2 tbsps of olive oil for 5 mins.
- Then add in the lemon zest, saffron, stock, parsley, and bay leafs.
- Get everything boiling, place a lid on the pot, set the heat to low, and cook the mix for 23 mins.
- At the same time begin heating 2 tbsps of olive, the onions, and the chicken for 7 mins.
- Then add the shrimp and cook the pieces of shrimp until they are done.
- Layer your rice in a casserole dish and layer the shrimp mix over everything.
- Enjoy.

Amount per serving (8 total)

Timing Information:

Preparation	30 m
Cooking	30 m
Total Time	1 h

Nutritional Information:

Calories	736 kcal
Fat	35.1 g
Carbohydrates	45.7g
Protein	55.7 g
Cholesterol	1202 mg
Sodium	1204 mg

* Percent Daily Values are based on a 2,000 calorie diet.

PICADILLO (LATIN BEEF HASH)

Ingredients

- 2 tbsps olive oil
- 1 lb ground beef
- 1/2 lb chorizo sausage, diced
- 1 large onion, diced
- 1/2 C. diced red bell pepper
- 2 cloves garlic, diced
- 1 tbsp ground cumin
- 2 tsps chili powder
- 1 tsp dried oregano
- 1 tsp paprika
- 1/4 tsp cayenne pepper
- 1/4 tsp ground cinnamon
- 1 1/2 C. canned diced tomatoes
- 3/4 C. beef stock
- 1 tbsp white sugar
- 1/2 C. raisins
- 1/4 C. diced pimento-stuffed green olives
- 2 tbsps apple cider vinegar
- 1 tbsp capers, drained
- 1/3 C. slivered almonds, toasted
- 1 tbsp lime juice

Directions

- Stir fry your chorizo and ground beef in olive oil for 12 mins.
- Remove most of the oils and add the bell peppers and onions.
- Cook the mix until everything is tender then add the garlic.

- Also add in: the cinnamon, cumin, cayenne, chili powder, paprika, and oregano.
- Fry this mix for 2 mins then add the beef stock, sugar, and the tomatoes.
- With a low level of heat gently boil the mix for 25 mins.
- Now add in the vinegar, raisins, capers, and olives.
- Let the contents cook for 7 mins.
- Now add the lime juice and the almonds.
- Make sure everything is hot.
- Enjoy.

Amount per serving (6 total)

Timing Information:

Preparation	15 m
Cooking	40 m
Total Time	55 m

Nutritional Information:

Calories	486 kcal
Fat	32.7 g
Carbohydrates	22.6g
Protein	25.5 g
Cholesterol	79 mg
Sodium	867 mg

* Percent Daily Values are based on a 2,000 calorie diet.

MONTEREY CHORIZO AND CHICKEN

Ingredients

- 1/4 lb chorizo
- 2 skinless, boneless chicken breast halves, cut into 1-inch cubes
- 1/2 (10 oz.) bag tortilla chips
- 1 C. frozen corn kernels
- 1 (19 oz.) can green enchilada sauce
- 1/2 C. sour cream
- 2 C. shredded Monterey Jack cheese

Directions

- Set your oven to 400 degrees before doing anything else.
- Fry your sausage and crumble it. Then add your pieces of chicken in the pan. Let the chicken and chorizo cook for 12 mins while stir frying.
- Get a bowl, combine: sour cream and enchilada sauce.
- Layer half of the chips in a baking dish then lay your chicken mix over the chips.
- Spread the corn, then add another layer of chips.
- Top everything with the sour cream mix.
- Then spread your cheese over the layers evenly and cook everything in oven for 17 mins. Enjoy.

Amount per serving (8 total)

Timing Information:

Preparation	15 m
Cooking	30 m
Total Time	45 m

Nutritional Information:

Calories	388 kcal
Fat	26 g
Carbohydrates	20.8g
Protein	19.4 g
Cholesterol	71 mg
Sodium	430 mg

* Percent Daily Values are based on a 2,000 calorie diet.

Italian Festival Sausage and Pepper

Ingredients

- 2 tsps vegetable oil
- 4 Buffalo wing-flavored chicken sausages (such as al fresco(R)), sliced
- 1 onion, sliced
- 1 red bell pepper, sliced
- 1 green bell pepper, sliced
- 1/4 C. blue cheese salad dressing, or more to taste
- 3 tbsps hot pepper sauce
- 2 C. baby spinach leaves
- 4 hoagie rolls, split lengthwise and toasted

Directions

- Fry your sausage in oil for 5 mins each side then combine in the bell pepper and onions.
- Let the peppers fry for 6 mins then place everything in a bowl when the sausage is completely done.
- Add the hot sauce and blue cheese to the sausage and stir the mix.
- Get your rolls, and layer some spinach on them evenly, then divide the sausage between the rolls.
- Enjoy.

Amount per serving (4 total)

Timing Information:

Preparation	15 m
Cooking	10 m
Total Time	25 m

Nutritional Information:

Calories	707 kcal
Fat	27.5 g
Carbohydrates	82.3g
Protein	30 g
Cholesterol	73 mg
Sodium	2226 mg

* Percent Daily Values are based on a 2,000 calorie diet.

INSTANT CABBAGE AND SAUSAGE

Ingredients

- 1 (4 oz.) package Instant Potatoes
- olive oil
- 1 (12 oz.) package chicken sausage, sliced
- 1 head cabbage, cut into 4 pieces, core removed
- 1 tbsp chicken stock
- 1 tbsp balsamic vinegar
- Sea salt
- Ground pepper
- 2 tbsps stone ground mustard

Directions

- Begin to fry your sausage in oil until they are fully done.
- Remove the sausages from the pot then add in the cabbage.
- Cook the cabbage until it is somewhat soft then pour in the chicken stock.
- Place a lid on the pot and let the cabbage fully cook.
- Combine the sausage back into the pot then add some pepper and salt.
- Now add the balsamic to the cabbage.
- Make your instant potatoes. Then add the mustard to the broth mix and stir everything. Enjoy.

Amount per serving (4 total)

Timing Information:

Preparation	15 m
Cooking	40 m
Total Time	55 m

Nutritional Information:

Calories	223 kcal
Fat	8.1 g
Carbohydrates	22.4g
Protein	16 g
Cholesterol	53 mg
Sodium	994 mg

* Percent Daily Values are based on a 2,000 calorie diet.

MEDITERRANEAN LAMB SAUSAGE BURGERS

Ingredients

- 1 tsp salt
- 1/4 tsp fennel seeds
- 1 tsp ground cumin
- 1/2 tsp ground cinnamon
- 1/2 tsp ground coriander
- 1/4 tsp ground turmeric
- 3 cloves garlic, peeled
- 2 tbsps harissa, or to taste (see Ingredient note)
- 1 tbsp tomato paste
- 1 lb lean ground lamb
- 1 tbsp olive oil

Directions

- Mash your fennel seeds and salt with a grinder then combine the mix with the following in a mortar and pestle: cloves, cumin, garlic cloves, cinnamon, turmeric, and coriander.
- Mash everything until it is smooth then add the mix to a bowl with the tomato paste and harissa.
- Get a 2nd bowl and mix the lamb with the spice mix then place a covering of plastic on the bowl.
- Put the bowl in the fridge for 8 hrs.
- Now shape the lamb into burgers and fry each one for 7 mins each side, in hot olive oil. Enjoy.

Amount per serving (4 total)

Timing Information:

Preparation	10 m
Cooking	10 m
Total Time	1 d 20 m

Nutritional Information:

Calories	280 kcal
Fat	19 g
Carbohydrates	6.5g
Protein	19.9 g
Cholesterol	76 mg
Sodium	743 mg

* Percent Daily Values are based on a 2,000 calorie diet.

SPRINGTIME SAUSAGE

Ingredients

- 5 lbs ground beef
- 5 tsps sugar-based curing mixture
- 1/4 C. mustard seed
- 3 tbsps garlic powder
- 1 tsp cayenne pepper
- 1 tbsp red pepper flakes
- 1 tbsp salt
- 1/2 tsp hickory-flavored liquid smoke

Directions

- Get a bowl, combine: liquid smoke, beef, salt, curing spice, pepper flakes, mustard seed, cayenne, and garlic powder.
- Combine the mix evenly then place a covering of plastic on the bowl and put everything in the fridge for 4 days.
- Combine the mix for 5 mins each day.
- Set your oven to 200 degrees. Then begin to form 5 sausages from the mix.
- Place the sausages into a casserole dish and cook them for 8 hrs.
- Once the sausages have cooled cover them with plastic and slice the pieces for serving with dishes.
- Enjoy.

Amount per serving (40 total)

Timing Information:

Preparation	10 m
Cooking	8 h
Total Time	3 d 8 h 10 m

Nutritional Information:

Calories	111 kcal
Fat	7.3 g
Carbohydrates	1g
Protein	< 10 g
Cholesterol	36 mg
Sodium	498 mg

* Percent Daily Values are based on a 2,000 calorie diet.

Homemade Vegetarian Sausages

Ingredients

- 1 1/2 C. vital wheat gluten flour
- 1/4 C. nutritional yeast
- 2 tsps mustard powder
- 2 tsps paprika
- 1 1/2 tsps crushed fennel seeds
- 1 tsp salt
- 1 tsp ground black pepper
- 1 tsp garlic powder
- 1 tsp cayenne pepper
- 1/2 tsp crushed anise seeds
- 1/2 tsp white sugar
- 3/4 C. cold water
- 1/4 C. tomato paste
- 2 tbsps olive oil
- 2 tbsps liquid amino acid (such as Bragg(R))
- 2 tsps liquid smoke flavoring

Directions

- Set your oven to 325 degrees before doing anything else.
- Get a bowl, combine: sugar, wheat flour, anise seeds, yeast, cayenne, mustard powder, garlic powder, paprika, black pepper, fennel, and salt.
- Get a 2nd bowl, combine: liquid smoke, water, amino acid, olive oil, and tomato paste.
- Combine both bowls and form a dense mix.

- Work the mix until it is smooth, on a cutting board, then shape everything into a cylinder with a height of 2 inches.
- Cover your sausage in foil then seal the edges.
- Cook everything in the oven for 1.5 hrs.
- Once the sausage has cooled, cut it into slices, or a shape you prefer for your dishes.
- Keep the sausage in the fridge wrapped in plastic for storage.
- Enjoy.

Amount per serving (12 total)

Timing Information:

Preparation	20 m
Cooking	1 h 30 m
Total Time	2 h 20 m

Nutritional Information:

Calories	113 kcal
Fat	3.4 g
Carbohydrates	8.7g
Protein	11.7 g
Cholesterol	0 mg
Sodium	349 mg

* Percent Daily Values are based on a 2,000 calorie diet.

CHINESE SAUSAGE DUMPLINGS

Ingredients

- 1 egg white
- 1 tbsp water
- 1 lb lean ground beef
- 1 lb bulk hot Italian sausage
- 1 tbsp Asian sweet chili sauce, or to taste
- 1 tbsp Chinese five-spice powder
- 1 tsp garlic powder
- 1 green onion, finely diced
- salt and pepper to taste
- 1 (16 oz.) package wonton wrappers
- 3 C. vegetable oil for frying
- 1/2 C. Asian sweet chili sauce, for dipping

Directions

- Get a bowl, combine: water and egg whites.
- Get a 2nd bowl, combine: pepper, beef, salt, sausage, green onions, 1 tbsp chili sauce, garlic powder, and five spice.
- Lay out your wrapper and add 1 tsp of mix then shape the wrapper into a dumpling and crimp the edges use the egg mix as a sealant.
- Begin to deep fry the dumplings in very hot oil for 5 mins.
- Top the wontons with the rest of the chili sauce or place the sauce to the side for dipping. Enjoy.

Amount per serving (12 total)

Timing Information:

Preparation	40 m
Cooking	15 m
Total Time	55 m

Nutritional Information:

Calories	338 kcal
Fat	17.5 g
Carbohydrates	27.6g
Protein	16.6 g
Cholesterol	50 mg
Sodium	641 mg

* Percent Daily Values are based on a 2,000 calorie diet.

CHINESE STYLE SAUSAGES IN A JAR

Ingredients

- 4 C. water
- 2 tbsps salt
- 4 C. distilled white vinegar
- 10 drops red food coloring (optional)
- 10 links smoked beef sausage, sliced into 3 pieces

Directions

- Get the following boiling in a saucepan: food coloring, water, vinegar, and salt.
- Get a big jar and add in your sausage pieces.
- Fill the jar with the vinegar mix then place the lid on the jar tightly.
- Leave the sausages for 2 days.
- Enjoy.

Amount per serving (10 total)

Timing Information:

Preparation	5 m
Cooking	5 m
Total Time	2 d 10 m

Nutritional Information:

Calories	136 kcal
Fat	11.6 g
Carbohydrates	1g
Protein	< 6.1 g
Cholesterol	29 mg
Sodium	1882 mg

* Percent Daily Values are based on a 2,000 calorie diet.

SAUSAGE APPLESAUCE APPETIZER

Ingredients

- 2 lbs Italian sausage
- 3/4 C. packed brown sugar
- 1 C. chunky applesauce
- 1 onion, diced

Directions

- Set your oven to 325 degrees before doing anything else.
- Fry your sausages until they are done then dice them.
- Place the meat in a baking dish then add in the onions, applesauce, and brown sugar.
- Stir the mix then cook everything for 50 mins.
- Enjoy.

Amount per serving (8 total)

Timing Information:

Preparation	10 m
Cooking	45 m
Total Time	55 m

Nutritional Information:

Calories	501 kcal
Fat	35.6 g
Carbohydrates	28.6g
Protein	16.4 g
Cholesterol	86 mg
Sodium	837 mg

* Percent Daily Values are based on a 2,000 calorie diet.

PORTUGUESE AND BRAZILIAN SAUSAGE SOUP

Ingredients

- 1 tbsp olive oil
- 3 stalks celery, diced
- 1 onion, diced
- 3 cloves garlic, diced
- 1 lb ground beef
- 1/2 lb spicy chorizo, casings removed and discarded
- 2 (28 oz.) cans tomato sauce
- 1 (14.5 oz.) can stewed tomatoes
- 1 (6 oz.) can tomato paste
- 1 (10 oz.) can diced tomatoes with green chile peppers
- 1 (1.25 oz.) package chili seasoning mix, or to taste

Directions

- Stir fry your garlic, onion, and celery in olive oil, in a saucepan for 9 mins. Add in the sausage and beef then crumble the meat as it fries for 12 mins.
- Add in the diced tomatoes and chilies, tomato sauce, tomato paste, and stewed tomatoes then stir the mix.
- Add in the chili powder then stir the mix gain.
- Get everything boiling, set the heat to low, and let the contents cook for 2 hrs. Enjoy.

Amount per serving (6 total)

Timing Information:

Preparation	20 m
Cooking	2 h
Total Time	2 h 20 m

Nutritional Information:

Calories	474 kcal
Fat	27.2 g
Carbohydrates	33.5g
Protein	29.1 g
Cholesterol	81 mg
Sodium	3013 mg

* Percent Daily Values are based on a 2,000 calorie diet.

CHEDDAR SMOKED POTATOES

Ingredients

- 2 tbsps olive oil
- 2 large russet potatoes, peeled and cut into 1-inch cubes
- 1 (14 oz.) beef smoked sausage, cut into 1/2-inch slices
- 2 (4 oz.) cans diced green chilies
- 2 C. shredded Cheddar cheese

Directions

- Fry your sausage and potatoes in olive oil for 12 mins then add in the chilies and cook everything for 7 more mins.
- Shut the heat and combine the mix with the cheddar.
- Place a lid on the pot and leave everything for 7 mins to melt the cheese.
- Enjoy.

Amount per serving (4 total)

Timing Information:

Preparation	15 m
Cooking	15 m
Total Time	30 m

Nutritional Information:

Calories	751 kcal
Fat	52.4 g
Carbohydrates	38.2g
Protein	32.3 g
Cholesterol	126 mg
Sodium	2141 mg

* Percent Daily Values are based on a 2,000 calorie diet.

SAUSAGE PASTRY

Ingredients

- 1 lb bulk breakfast sausage
- 1 (16 oz.) package shredded mozzarella cheese
- 1/2 C. grated Parmesan cheese
- 1 egg
- 1 (16 oz.) package refrigerated pizza dough
- 1 egg yolk, beaten

Directions

- Set your oven to 350 degrees before doing anything else.
- Stir fry your sausage for 12 mins then remove them from the pot.
- Get a bowl, combine: egg, sausage, parmesan, and mozzarella.
- Shape your dough into a rectangle and place it on a cookie sheet.
- Top the dough with the cheese mix and roll it up.
- Crimp the seal to close everything and coat the rolls with the beaten yolk.
- Cook the roll in the oven for 65 mins.
- Once the sausage roll has lost its heat cut it into servings.
- Enjoy.

Amount per serving (12 total)

Timing Information:

Preparation	15 m
Cooking	1 h 10 m
Total Time	1 h 40 m

Nutritional Information:

Calories	315 kcal
Fat	17.2 g
Carbohydrates	19.2g
Protein	19.6 g
Cholesterol	81 mg
Sodium	878 mg

* Percent Daily Values are based on a 2,000 calorie diet.

JALAPENO SAUSAGE PASTRY

Ingredients

- 2 lbs pork sausage (such as Jimmy Dean(R))
- 1 onion, finely diced
- 1 (8 oz.) package cream cheese, softened
- 2 jalapeno peppers, seeded and finely diced
- 4 (8 oz.) packages crescent roll dough, unrolled and divided into triangles

Directions

- Fry your sausage for 8 mins then remove any excess oils.
- Get a bowl, combine: jalapenos, sausage, cream cheese, and onions.
- Layer 1 tbsp of sausage mix on your pieces of dough then shape the dough into a crescent.
- Layer everything into a casserole dish and cook them in the oven for 20 mins.
- Enjoy.

Amount per serving (32 total)

Timing Information:

Preparation	20 m
Cooking	15 m
Total Time	35 m

Nutritional Information:

Calories	210 kcal
Fat	14.5 g
Carbohydrates	12.1g
Protein	6.5 g
Cholesterol	24 mg
Sodium	494 mg

* Percent Daily Values are based on a 2,000 calorie diet.

Breakfast Muffins

Ingredients

- 1 (9.6 oz.) box pre-cooked sausage links
- 2 3/4 C. all-purpose flour*
- 1 (.25 oz.) envelope Fleischmann's(R) RapidRise Yeast
- 2 tbsps sugar
- 1 tsp salt
- 1 C. very warm milk
- 1 tbsp corn oil
- 1 egg
- 1 tsp vanilla extract
- 2 tbsps sugar
- 1/2 tsp ground Cinnamon
- 2 tbsps butter
- Pancake syrup

Directions

- Get your sausage hot and cut them into slices.
- Now add the following to the bowl of a stand mixer: salt, 1.5 C. flour, sugar, undissolved yeast.
- Then add in the vanilla, milk, eggs, and oil.
- Mix everything for 3 mins at the medium level. Then slowly combine in the rest of the flour to create a dough.
- Now combine in the sausage pieces.
- Place a covering on the bowl of plastic and let the dough sit for 15 mins.

- Set your oven to 375 degrees before doing anything else.
- Divide the dough evenly between 12 sections of a muffin tin then place a kitchen towel over the dough again and let the dough sit for 40 mins.
- Get a bowl and combine cinnamon and sugar.
- Cook the muffins in the oven for 30 mins then top them with butter and sugar mix.
- When eating the muffins divide them in half and top each half with a bit of syrup.
- Enjoy.

Amount per serving (12 total)

Timing Information:

Preparation	10 m
Cooking	1 h 30 m
Total Time	1 h 40 m

Nutritional Information:

Calories	255 kcal
Fat	12.9 g
Carbohydrates	28.1g
Protein	7.2 g
Cholesterol	36 mg
Sodium	439 mg

* Percent Daily Values are based on a 2,000 calorie diet.

MIDSUMMER SAUSAGE WITH CRANBERRIES AND WALNUTS

Ingredients

- 1/2 (12 oz.) package fresh cranberries
- 1 lb sausage
- 6 C. bread cubes
- 1 C. seasoned dry bread crumbs
- 1 medium onion, diced
- 1 clove garlic, minced
- 1 tsp diced fresh parsley
- 1/2 tsp diced fresh oregano
- 1/2 tsp diced fresh sage
- 1 pinch fresh thyme
- 1/3 tsp celery seed
- 1/4 tsp ground ginger
- 1/2 tsp salt
- 1/3 tsp ground black pepper
- 2 C. reduced sodium chicken broth
- 1/2 C. diced walnuts
- 1/2 C. diced orange with skin on

Directions

- Get your cranberries boiling in water. Once the skins begin to bubble remove all the liquids.
- Fry your sausages until they are done then remove the oils.
- Set your oven to 350 degrees before doing anything else.

- Place the following into a casserole dish: garlic, cranberries, onion, sausage, bread crumbs, and bread cubes.
- Add in the pepper, salt, parsley, ginger, oregano, celery seed, thyme, and sage.
- Stir the mix then add in the broth.
- Stir the mix again then add the orange and walnut.
- Cook everything in the oven for 30 mins.
- Enjoy.

Amount per serving (10 total)

Timing Information:

Preparation	30 m
Cooking	25 m
Total Time	1 h 15 m

Nutritional Information:

Calories	351 kcal
Fat	23.6 g
Carbohydrates	24.7g
Protein	10.5 g
Cholesterol	32 mg
Sodium	797 mg

* Percent Daily Values are based on a 2,000 calorie diet.

ANTIPASTO

Ingredients

- 1 lb seashell pasta
- 1/4 lb Genoa salami, diced
- 1/4 lb pepperoni sausage, diced
- 1/2 lb Asiago cheese, diced
- 1 (6 oz.) can black olives, drained and diced
- 1 red bell pepper, diced
- 1 green bell pepper, diced
- 3 tomatoes, diced
- 1 (.7 oz.) package dry Italian-style salad dressing mix
- 3/4 C. extra virgin olive oil
- 1/4 C. balsamic vinegar
- 2 tbsps dried oregano
- 1 tbsp dried parsley
- 1 tbsp grated Parmesan cheese
- salt and ground black pepper to taste

Directions

- Boil your pasta in water and salt for 9 mins then remove all the liquids.
- Get a bowl, combine: tomatoes, pasta, bell peppers, salami, olives, pepperoni, and asiago.
- Place a covering of plastic around the mix and put everything in the fridge for 65 mins.

- Get a 2nd bowl, combine: black pepper, olive oil, salt, balsamic, parmesan, parsley, and oregano.
- Combine both bowls, once the pasta mix is cold and toss the contents.
- Enjoy.

Amount per serving (12 total)

Timing Information:

Preparation	20 m
Cooking	15 m
Total Time	1 h 35 m

Nutritional Information:

Calories	451 kcal
Fat	29.1 g
Carbohydrates	33.2g
Protein	15 g
Cholesterol	37 mg
Sodium	978 mg

* Percent Daily Values are based on a 2,000 calorie diet.

SHEFTALIA

(TANGY GREEK ONIONS AND SAUSAGE)

Ingredients

- 1 lb. ground pork
- 1 large onion, finely chopped
- 1/2 C. finely chopped fresh parsley
- 1 pinch salt and pepper to taste
- 1 tbsp vinegar
- 1/2 lb. caul fat
- 10 skewers

Directions

- Get a bowl, combine: pepper, pork, salt, onions, and parsley.
- Get a 2nd bowl and add in vinegar and warm water.
- Add the caul to the water and leave it submerged for 3 mins.
- Now cut the caul into 4" rectangles. Add an equal amount of pork meat to each caul and then roll each one up. Continue until you have 10 sausages. Stake a skewer through each sausage and grill them for 22 mins. Flip each piece at least 4 times throughout the cooking time.
- Let the sausage cool before serving. Enjoy.

Amount per serving (3 total)

Timing Information:

Preparation	1 h
Cooking	1 h
Total Time	2 h

Nutritional Information:

Calories	1070 kcal
Fat	103.4 g
Carbohydrates	15.7g
Protein	27.7 g
Cholesterol	160 mg
Sodium	226 mg

* Percent Daily Values are based on a 2,000 calorie diet.

EASY BANGERS AND MASH

Ingredients

- 8 large baking potatoes, peeled and quartered
- 2 tsps butter, divided
- 1/2 C. milk, or as needed
- salt and pepper to taste

- 1 1/2 lbs beef sausage
- 1/2 C. diced onion
- 1 (.75 oz.) packet dry brown gravy mix
- 1 C. water, or as needed

Directions

- Set your oven to 350 degrees before doing anything else.
- For 20 mins boil your potatoes in water. Remove all the water and mash them. Then add in: salt, milk, pepper, and 1 tsp of butter. Mash again.
- Fry your sausage in a pan and then set them to the side and fry your onions in 1 tsp of butter.
- Combine water and gravy in the same pan and let the contents lightly boil. Continue boiling the gravy until thick.
- Now get a baking dish and line the bottom of it with some gravy and onions. Then cut your sausages in half and put them on top of the gravy. Add the potatoes over the sausages and then the remaining gravy.
- Cook in the oven for 23 mins. Enjoy.

Amount per serving (8 total)

Timing Information:

Preparation	15 m
Cooking	45 m
Total Time	1 h

Nutritional Information:

Calories	570 kcal
Fat	24.9 g
Carbohydrates	67.7g
Protein	20.3 g
Cholesterol	61 mg
Sodium	1206 mg

* Percent Daily Values are based on a 2,000 calorie diet.

THANKS FOR READING! NOW LET'S TRY SOME **SUSHI** AND **DUMP DINNERS**....

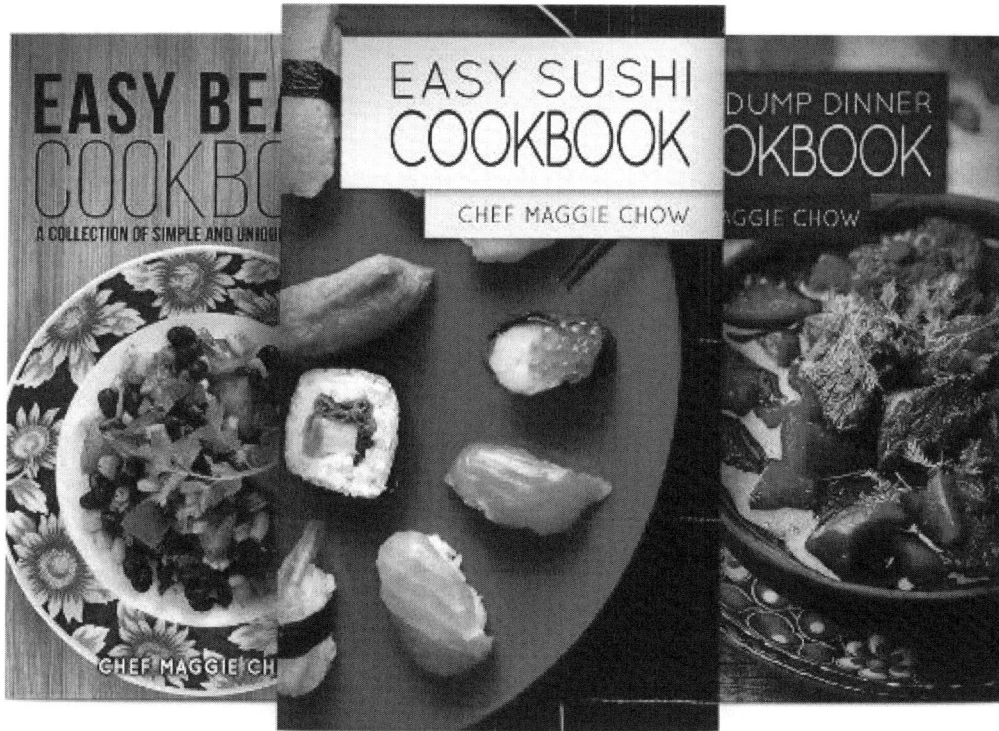

<u>Send the Book!</u>

To grab this **box set** simply follow the link mentioned above, or tap the book cover.

This will take you to a page where you can simply enter your email address and a PDF version of the **box set** will be emailed to you.

I hope you are ready for some serious cooking!

Send the Book!

You will also receive updates about all my new books when they are free.

Also don't forget to like and subscribe on the social networks. I love meeting my readers. Links to all my profiles are below so please click and connect :)

Facebook

Twitter

Come On...
Let's Be Friends :)

I adore my readers and love connecting with them socially. Please follow the links below so we can connect on Facebook, Twitter, and Google+.

Facebook

Twitter

I also have a blog that I regularly update for my readers so check it out below.

My Blog

CAN I ASK A FAVOUR?

If you found this book interesting, or have otherwise found any benefit in it. Then may I ask that you post a review of it on Amazon? Nothing excites me more than new reviews, especially reviews which suggest new topics for writing. I do read all reviews and I always factor feedback into my newer works.

So if you are willing to take ten minutes to write what you sincerely thought about this book then please visit our Amazon page and post your opinions.

Again thank you!

Interested in Other Easy Cookbooks?

Everything is easy! Check out my Amazon Author page for more great cookbooks:

For a complete listing of all my books please see my author page.

Printed in Great Britain
by Amazon